Our Snowman

First published in 2010
by Wayland

Text copyright © Cynthia Rider
Illustration copyright © Nicola Evans

Wayland
338 Euston Road
London NW1 3BH

Wayland Australia
Level 17/207 Kent Street
Sydney, NSW 2000

Series Editor: Louise John
Editor: Katie Powell
Cover design: Paul Cherrill
Design: D.R.ink
Consultant: Shirley Bickler

A CIP catalogue record for this book is available from the British Library.

ISBN 9780750260602

Printed in China

Wayland is a division of Hachette Children's Books,
an Hachette UK Company

www.hachette.co.uk

Our Snowman

Written by Cynthia Rider
Illustrated by Nicola Evans

WAYLAND

Look!

We are making a snowman.

Look!

We are making a snowman
with a big red nose.

Look!

We are making a snowman

with big black eyes.

8

9

Look!

We are making a snowman
with a big orange mouth.

Look!

We are making a snowman with big blue buttons.

Look!

We are making a snowman
with big yellow gloves.

Look!

We are making a snowman
with a big green scarf.

Look!

We are making a snowman
with a big brown hat.

Look at our
big snowman!

21

Guiding a First Read of
Our Snowman

It is important to talk through the book with the child before they read it alone. This prepares them for the way the story unfolds, and allows them to enjoy the pictures as you both talk naturally, using the language they will later encounter when reading. Read them the brief overview, and then follow the suggestions below:

1. Talking through the book
This book's about a snowman. The children are finishing making its body and its head, and now they are decorating the snowman to make it very colourful.

Let's read the title: **Our Snowman.**
Turn to page 4. The children say, "Look! We are making a snowman."
On page 6 they say, "Look! We are making a snowman with a big red nose."
What do you think they say on page 8? Yes, "Look! We are making a snowman with big black eyes."

Continue through the book, guiding the discussion to fit the text as the child looks at the illustrations.

On page 18 they finish off the snowman with a big brown hat. What do they say?
And on the last page, they say, "Look at our big snowman!"

2. A first reading of the book

Ask the child to read the book independently, pointing carefully under each word (tracking), while thinking about the story. Praise attempts by the child to correct themselves, and prompt them to use their letter knowledge, the punctuation and check the meaning, for example:

> **That word says 'with'. Say it slowly and look at it carefully, 'w i th'. Now try that page again. Did that make sense?**

> **You said, "We made a snowman." Then you went back and changed it to, "We are making a snowman." Is that right now? That was really good checking.**

> **I like the way you make 'big' sound really big!**

3. Follow-up activities

The high frequency words in this title are:

a   are   at   big   we   with

- Select a new high frequency word, and ask the child to find it throughout the book. Discuss the shape of the letters and the letter sounds.
- To memorise the word, ask the child to write it in the air, then write it repeatedly on a whiteboard or on paper, leaving a space between each attempt.

4. Encourage

- Reading the book again – with expression.
- Drawing a picture based on the story.
- Writing one or two sentences using the practised words.

START READING is a series of highly enjoyable books for beginner readers. **The books have been carefully graded to match the Book Bands widely used in schools.** This enables readers to be sure they choose books that match their own reading ability.

Look out for the Band colour on the book in our Start Reading logo.

The Bands are:

Pink Band 1A & 1B

Red Band 2

Yellow Band 3

Blue Band 4

Green Band 5

Orange Band 6

Turquoise Band 7

Purple Band 8

Gold Band 9

START READING books can be read independently or shared with an adult. They promote the enjoyment of reading through satisfying stories supported by fun illustrations.

Cynthia Rider lives in the Peak District of Derbyshire and often finds inspiration for her stories in the countryside around her. She particularly enjoys writing for young children and encouraging their love of reading.

Nicola Evans works as a freelance illustrator in a small village on the south coast of England, where she lives with her husband and three-year-old daughter. She loves illustrating for children, helping to bring books alive with her characters and colours.